Doctor Rashid Buttar ~ MEDICAL DOCTOR

&Thoughts of mine having watched one of his videos in particular on youtube (A VIDEO THAT Youtube has now removed)

Introduction

Look back over your shoulder at all of my thus far book titles and tell me what you see: what is it you see? A diamond full of light or a piece of West Virginia coal? What is it you see? Tell me. Is it real or imagined or can you tell if it's something buried in time past or something that is yet to come? Can you tell me what it actually is right now in all of its varied aspects? And if so, how

Part 1. Base Camp

Yes, look back over your shoulder at all my "thus far" book titles. No. this isn't a greatest hits or sum of that I'm talking about - of all I've ever written - But "it is what it is" = A sum total view of all I'm saying here in every book and all I've ever said live to a face I was face to face with.

When I was there at a place in my memory. A place that had been built in 1956. It looked like what it was: a construction of wood boards and post and sheets of galvanized tin that someone I knew who'd taken thought for animals had constructed there on His post World War2 Farm that existed in the not so deep South that you

could tell was what
is meant or invoked
into the minds of
people when they hear
words sewn together
in such a way as to
say "the deep south".
And I step into a
boat that no one
around me can see and
that's when / what I
do is need to go back
to that place, where
this individual was
situated there on
that post World War 2
farm and the boards
and tin were part of

His farm that he shared with his brother. And I step out of that boat that has me carried back to that place and I'm putting everything into reverse in real-life memories.

Now today. What is going on in USA? In the place that Thomas Jefferson wrote so eloquently about? Saying / teaching the USA Citizens populous then and today as his words echo through time from then until now on this shore we all stand upon in USA who are its citizens and there is a knocking on the door of USA with axes of the Communist who are included in who we know he was warning of that didn't exist by that name then but did exist in the kind of people who are opposite of what the founding fathers in

USA wrote its citizens / likeminded populous of = those who'd try to suppress your life: by saying you cannot speak about certain things or go where you wanted to travel to nor worship God as you desired nor defend yourself nor your family nor any good person against tyrants, who would and they knew they would, would rear their ugly heads in the USA government.

There at that wood and tin shelter on that farm the old man went to from time to time for a handful of cherry tomatoes but most the time it was his brother and there at that wood and tin shelter which for sake of description right here I will refer to as the name they called it, the hog lot, I see Joe take a pig and throw it back between his legs with its face where he could look straight at it, then, he took a pair of clippers such as would clip a 10 gauge steel wire in half with no problem and clip the pigs teeth off and then clip its tail off and then take a straight cold steel razor blade and having turned the pig around so that he now looks upon it's rear, if it was a male pig, he’d cut the testicles off from that pigs scrotum and let them drop there on the ground where a cat or dog could easily pass by and snack on them, and then finally he took a big needle and having filled the shot with iron he’d inject the pig with it and then put him back down on the ground where he’d go back to his mother who was communicating with him as he squealed the entire time that had been happening to him. And why had that happened to him? Well, as I was told it was to make the pigs as they grew up to not become like pigs without this having been done to them would do which is to grow long tails and teeth and without their testicles they'd have control over the mind

of who had been a
male who they really
only wanted to fatten
up with feed to eat
and then when they'd
been a certain age to
be taken to market
and sold for money
for the farm for this
was their livelihood
being farmers there
in the deep south.
But I say deep-south
like I would say
pecan or tomato or
potato or butter
pecan ice cream or
huckleberry.

There standing in the boat I am just looking at all they did and how whenever it was that the doors of their Southern Baptist Church was / were open they were there. And I smell the country ham and eggs and grits and toast and juice and coffee of their quarterly Sunday morning breakfasts. Yeah, I'm there too with them for I was always right there with them. When? When they were here in the land of the living and we were all together in that tight knit community.

Ok. Let's think / reason together: If "IF" they were in the Second World War in the army or merchant marines or whatever… [Thinking] …were they so close to the conspiracy (or plan that the world elites have to the point that they war people against each other… Nations on a large scale or even individuals on a much reduced scale… to the point that "they" actually make the pieces of the game to be played (such as weapons of war) before-hand knowing that this is just what they do being in this fallen world and serving who it is that they serve?

Ok. Here we go again.

We all have our own individual pasts.

We all know where it is that we've come from and have a point of view about it and about others aspects of having been born in the USA.

We know what it was like when we were kids and those who had been in the Second World War heard us as we played war. Some of us red coats and some of us blue coats and some of us American and some of us German and some of playing the part of Japan. Right. We were English or French or Indian allies of one of them or another of them.

Why was it this way?
That we followed the
ways of this fallen
world?

And why was it that
in the Church they
even said "this" type
of behavior was ok?

I tell you what,
unless you have lived
enough years you have
no wisdom to
understand what it is
that the old men
understand who've
lived long enough to

be able to. I'm especially talking about those who are in the church who've progressed far enough ahead of the younger generation to finally be able to understand.

Understand what?

Well, to understand what it is a Kingdom of God Citizen should understand, if he or she were disciple

according to
Scripture in the
Right way.

The Right Way?

Yes, the Right Way.
That is to say,
according to
Scripture.

But you're implying
that even within the
church that the
church itself has
become a filter
through which

everyone flows (everyone who is in the church flows through…)

And then… out into the world and the world's ways: practicing the world ways even though they are in the church they have become "They".

Yes. That's right.

The Church isn’t teaching people to follow the Good Shepherd of Scripture in my view. And thus confusing the line between who is God and who is Uncle Sam.

Hm. Ok. I hear you. Go on. Tell me more please.

Ok. I will but first remember that what I’m mentioning here is only like walking on thin ice, that, there is a whole deep ocean of facts behind everything I'm saying and you "You" (meaning people in general or any person in general) will have to do your own research for my books don't go that deep but they alert you to where the buoy is in the bay and from there you'll have to, having used that buoy as a marker, you'll have to chart your own course of discovering more about the subjects I'm referring to.

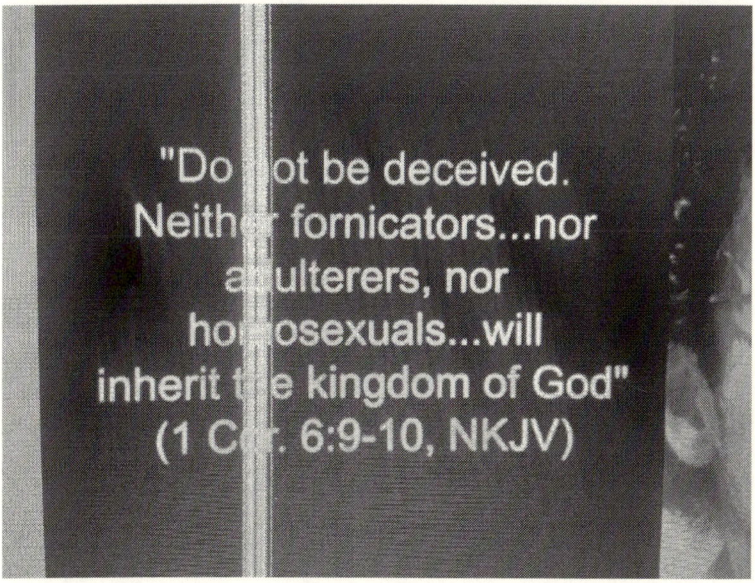

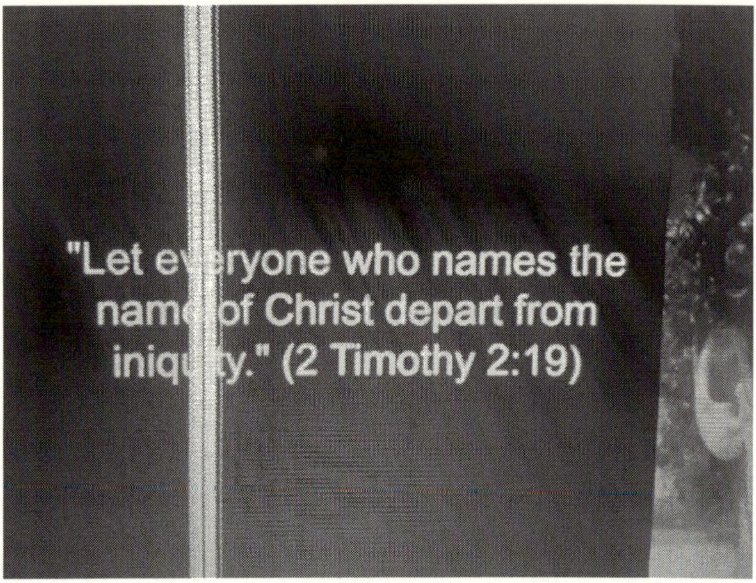
"Let everyone who names the
name of Christ depart from
iniquity." (2 Timothy 2:19)

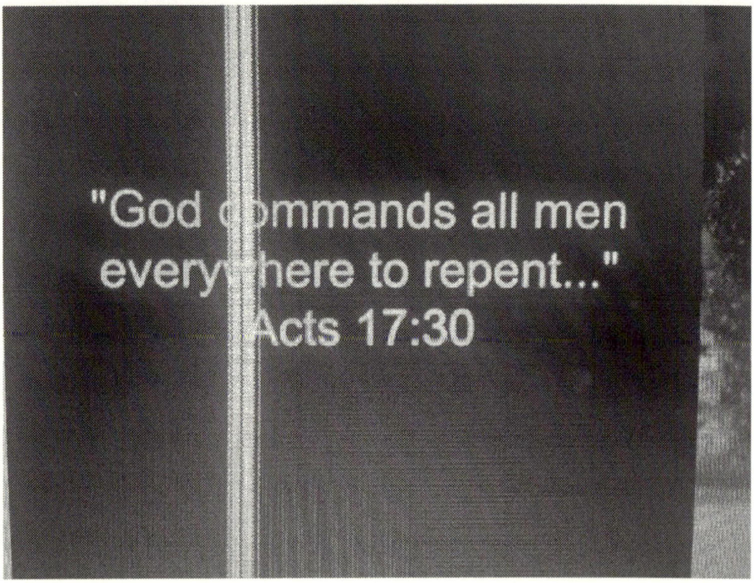
"God commands all men
everywhere to repent..."
Acts 17:30

Revelation 12:7-
17 King James Version
(KJV)
7 And there was war in
heaven: Michael and
his angels fought
against the dragon;
and the dragon fought
and his angels,

8 And prevailed not;
neither was their
place found any more
in heaven.

9 And the great dragon
was cast out, that
old serpent, called
the Devil, and Satan,
which deceived the

whole world: he was
cast out into the
earth, and his angels
were cast out with
him.

10 And I heard a loud
voice saying in
heaven, Now is come
salvation, and
strength, and the
kingdom of our God,
and the power of his
Christ: for the
accuser of our
brethren is cast
down, which accused
them before our God
day and night.

11 And they overcame
him by the blood of
the Lamb, and by the
word of their
testimony; and they
loved not their lives
unto the death.

12 Therefore rejoice,
ye heavens, and ye
that dwell in them.
Woe to the
inhabitor's of the
earth and of the sea!
For the devil is come
down unto you, having
great wrath, because
he knoweth that he
hath but a short
time.

13 And when the dragon
saw that he was cast
unto the earth, he
persecuted the woman
which brought forth
the man child.

14 And to the woman
were given two wings
of a great eagle,
that she might fly
into the wilderness,
into her place, where
she is nourished for
a time, and times,
and half a time, from
the face of the
serpent.

15 And the serpent
cast out of his mouth

water as a flood
after the woman, that
he might cause her to
be carried away of
the flood.

16 And the earth
helped the woman, and
the earth opened her
mouth, and swallowed
up the flood which
the dragon cast out
of his mouth.

17 And the dragon was
wroth with the woman,
and went to make war
with the remnant of
her seed, which keep
the commandments of
God, and have the

testimony of Jesus Christ.

Part 2. Into The Jungle

Ok. Got it.

Good. Then, do your own research on what Doctor Rashid Buttar says about the Coroa19 Virus and what he says about what's going on in the USA with the personalities of Bill Gates, Elon Musk, George Soros, Doctor Anthony Fauci, and the like. And do your research on 5G and contrast all of this against the Document:

COMMUNIST RULES OF REVOLUTION. And research who Hillary Clinton and President of United States Obama actually are; what they actually believe and are laboring in governments of the world to accomplish and research Saul Alinsky document How to Create a Socialist State and how that philosophy of theirs is being perpetuated upon an unsuspecting world today.

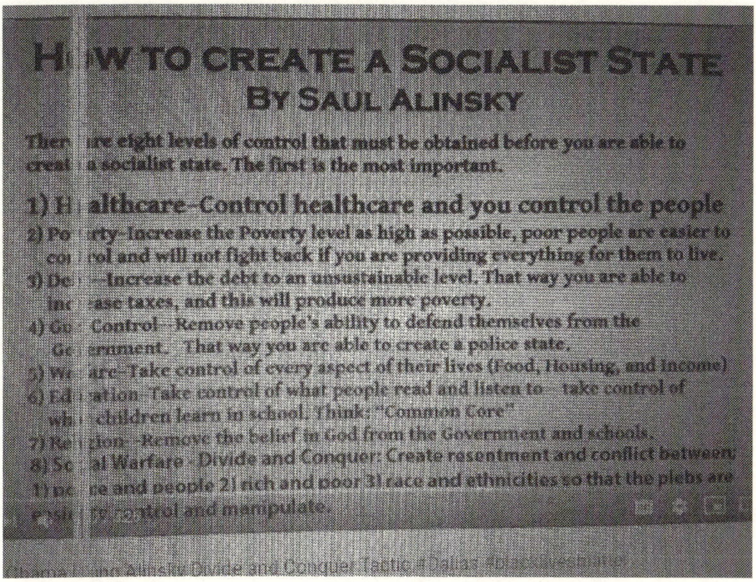

Also read the book En Route to Global Occupation by Gary H. Hah.

Also Levin (on Fox News): The Media is Using Covid Numbers to Mislead You.

Ok.

Now with that said: I had a conversation with a man who I will merely recount here pervade a conversation that is simple / and about what a lot of people are talking about in their day to day lives as "what is happening to all of us in the world today" are talking about or wondering to themselves about what it is that's actually going on:

A Conversation:

A person = "David" text:

"The Truth Is Learned, Never Told", Countdown To Treason, Blackout Coming.

[4:50 AM, 4/15/2020] Perris Jackson: "they" are destroying USA constitution

[4:51 AM, 4/15/2020] Perris Jackson: Trump said they wouldn't or he wouldn't allow them to ever do what they are doing

[4:52 AM, 4/15/2020] Perris Jackson: I see it like this right now: that they have shut down world economies En Route to Global Occupation

[7:19 PM, 4/15/2020] David Deeds: DS is still trying to screw up Trump

[7:21 PM, 4/15/2020] Perris Jackson: I've heard that he has no power , that he has been stripped of power and others are "telling him what to do" I even heard Joe Biden say someone had told him to call the white house and talk to trump and that he called and they talked and he had told him to do certain things.

[7:23 PM, 4/15/2020] Perris Jackson: "They" whoever they are destroying USA it seems

[7:23 PM, 4/15/2020] David xxxxx: it's the DS

[7:23 PM, 4/15/2020] Perris Jackson: Stripping citizens of constitution right

[7:23 PM, 4/15/2020] Perris Jackson: Who is DS?

[7:23 PM, 4/15/2020] David xxxxx: Democrats

[7:24 PM, 4/15/2020] Perris Jackson: Oh ok

[7:24 PM, 4/15/2020] David xxxxx: deep

state = Democrats...Clinton, bushes, Obama and their mittens

[7:25 PM, 4/15/2020] Perris Jackson: Well, it seems Hillary nor bidden, nor come, nor the like will not ever "be brought to justice"

[7:25 PM, 4/15/2020] Perris Jackson: Did bush senior play part on assassination of JFK

[7:26 PM, 4/15/2020] David xxxxx: we may not see them brought to justice, but they may just disappear

[7:26 PM, 4/15/2020] David xxxxx: hell yes

[7:26 PM, 4/15/2020] Perris Jackson: Yes. How could he not have?

[7:27 PM, 4/15/2020] David xxxxx: AS much as the Democrats try to stop the reopening of the US, they can't

[7:27 PM, 4/15/2020] David xxxxx: remember he was head of the CIA

[7:29 PM, 4/15/2020] David xxxxx: ALL the corruption within our government goes back 50 yrs. or more, Clinton and Obama have committed treason

[7:29 PM, 4/15/2020] Perris Jackson: I remember

[7:30 PM, 4/15/2020] David xxxxx: and that

will be proven I have no doubt on that

[7:30 PM, 4/15/2020] Perris Jackson: Right. I know and been protected to do so

[7:31 PM, 4/15/2020] Perris Jackson: But I think JFK was about to expose their plan to do what is going on today and not play along with their evil plan and "they"

murdered him

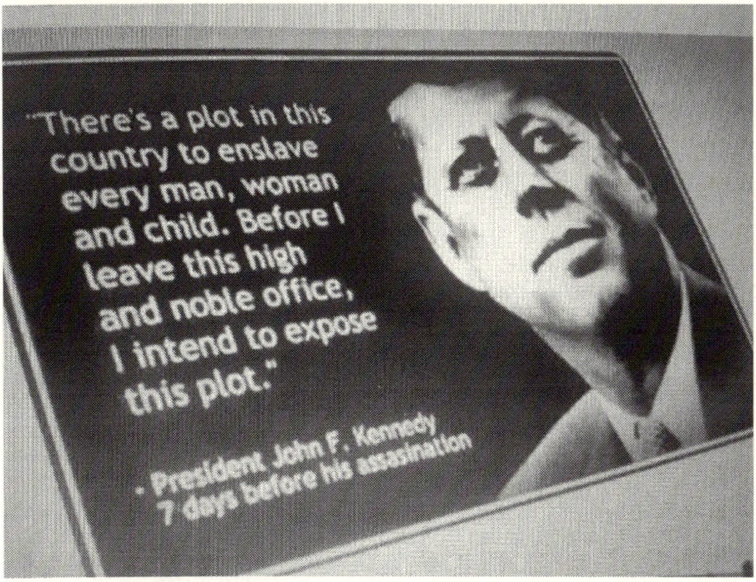

[7:32 PM, 4/15/2020] David xxxxx: the corruption ran so deep in the Obama adm and the executive order he wrote the day before Trump took office has been found

[7:32 PM, 4/15/2020] Perris Jackson: And I think that's why they almost murdered Reagan

and after that near assassination I think Reagan vice president bush ran the country

[7:33 PM, 4/15/2020] Perris Jackson: What executive order?

[7:33 PM, 4/15/2020] David xxxxx: all the media hype on this virus is being fan by the Democrats to delay the truth from coming out

[7:34 PM, 4/15/2020] David xxxxx: research Obama executive order last day in office, it's been on the net

[7:35 PM, 4/15/2020] Perris Jackson:

Right. That's right. Or it's been in their playbook and those behind the scenes who are contributors to "it" are "merely running the program"

[7:35 PM, 4/15/2020] David xxxxx: but they are being shut down too

[7:35 PM, 4/15/2020] Perris Jackson: Hopefully. And...

[7:36 PM, 4/15/2020] Perris Jackson: I saw

on news USA ships are in Gulf of Mexico

[7:36 PM, 4/15/2020] Perris Jackson: To not allow certain attacks on USA or something

[7:36 PM, 4/15/2020] David xxxxx: sometimes you have to let the rats expose their handlers

[7:36 PM, 4/15/2020] David xxxxx: ok there you go

[7:37 PM, 4/15/2020] David xxxxx: screw the DEMOCRATS

[7:38 PM, 4/15/2020] Perris Jackson: Yeah

[7:38 PM, 4/15/2020] David xxxxx: IF they get control of America, we lose our country

[8:02 PM, 4/15/2020] Perris Jackson: Yeah but I also realize that china is a USA creation , a template of what they want the whole world (NWO) to look like and it's been being built for decades and china may even launch nuclear strike against USA if "they" feel they have to in order to bring

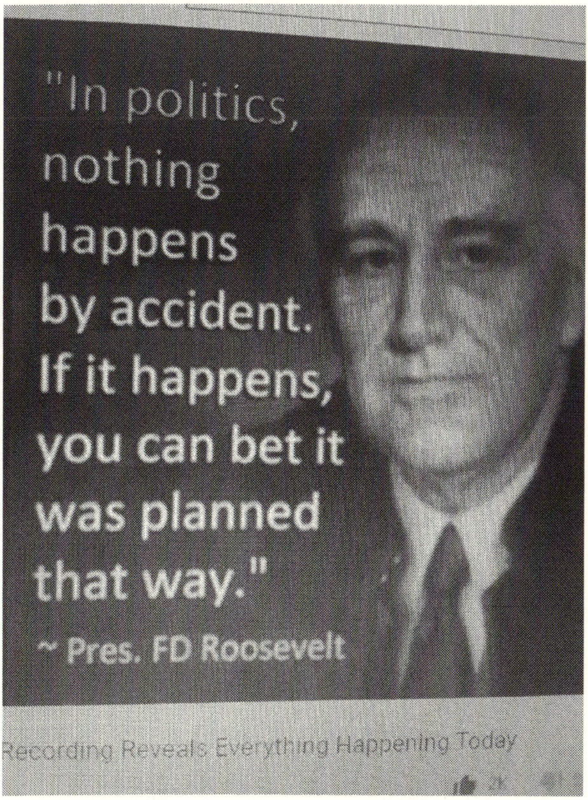

New World Order about, that , they wouldn't let JFK try and stop them nor will they stop short of achieving their goal of NWO, even if it means so much radioactive fallout is falling on USA that virtually nothing survives. And it's not china as a country but a puppet being moved by a hand we haven't actually seen as of yet

[8:13 PM, 4/15/2020] David xxxxx: want happen

[8:15 PM, 4/15/2020] Perris Jackson: I hope not

[8:15 PM, 4/15/2020] Perris Jackson: But it may be something else but just as catastrophic to USA

[8:16 PM, 4/15/2020] Perris Jackson: Why? Because the enemies of USA are within the USA government

[8:16 PM, 4/15/2020] Perris Jackson: Traitors

[8:20 PM, 4/15/2020] David xxxxx: Trump is in office and the White hats are with him

[8:29 PM, 4/15/2020] Perris Jackson: Even Nixon played a part. Here meeting with Mao for a week in 1972.

And when "they" were done with him he didn't wait to go through being impeached, instead he resigned and got out fast as he could because he knew what "they" did to JFK. Yes. It's been in the serious-works more than 50 years. Even back to creation of Federal Reserve

[8:30 PM, 4/15/2020] David xxxxx: true another crook

[8:31 PM, 4/15/2020] Perris Jackson: Nixon shaking hands of the ultimate God Hater: chairman Mao. And that's part of the plan they'd had then that has progressed to where it is today. Nixon was obviously doing his part. He obviously was as guilty of murdering JFK has every other like-minded deep state player. Such as Bill and Hillary Clinton and the like

Right but rather than what could have come out in a trial to

impeach him - he resigned before "they" murdered him too for fear of what could be said in a trial that led back to them

[8:32 PM, 4/15/2020] David xxxxx: true

[8:33 PM, 4/15/2020] David xxxxx: but he died and it wasn't from natural causes

[8:33 PM, 4/15/2020] Perris Jackson: Yes. I agree. But no one talks about the truth

and I think most know what is happening

[8:34 PM, 4/15/2020] David xxxxx: truth

has been hidden for a hundred yrs. what has been going on until now

[8:34 PM, 4/15/2020] Perris Jackson: Right

[8:36 PM, 4/15/2020] David xxxxx: a lot will never come to light

[8:41 PM, 4/15/2020] Perris Jackson: Right. I agree. And those puppet masters will be in their underground bunkers when "they" have destroyed the world which is really all they want to do for that is what their father , the evil one, has always only planned, knowing he has been de-throned.

[8:41 PM, 4/15/2020] David xxxxx: it's all about the $$$

[8:42 PM, 4/15/2020] Perris Jackson: For the one on the white horse has qualified to rule.

[8:43 PM, 4/15/2020] David xxxxx: yep

[8:51 PM, 4/15/2020] David xxxxx: true

[8:52 PM, 4/15/2020] Perris Jackson: Yes

[8:52 PM, 4/15/2020] Perris Jackson: I agree

[8:53 PM, 4/15/2020] David xxxxx: JFK Jr discovered who was behind is death and was also killed before he could expose them

[8:54 PM, 4/15/2020] David xxxxx: and trump has that info too

[8:55 PM, 4/15/2020] Perris Jackson: Yes. I think I saw where or read in an article which I can find again if so, that, the Clintons orchestrated his murder.

[8:56 PM, 4/15/2020] Perris Jackson: Ok. I remember

[8:56 PM, 4/15/2020] David xxxxx: ok, I promised I would never tell, that's no lie

[8:57 PM, 4/15/2020] Perris Jackson: Hillary was running for the same government office

[8:57 PM, 4/15/2020] Perris Jackson: And they murdered him

[8:57 PM, 4/15/2020] Perris Jackson: Before she had to run against him

[8:59 PM, 4/15/2020] David xxxxx: I KNOW TO MUCH AND SEEN WAY MORE THAN I SHOULD HAVE SEEN

[8:59 PM, 4/15/2020] Perris Jackson: Claim: "JFK Jr was declared the frontrunner for the NY Senate seat in 1999. Days later his plane crashed"

[9:00 PM, 4/15/2020] Perris Jackson: Ok

[9:05 PM, 4/15/2020] David xxxxx: IT WAS MADE TO CRASH

That was part of a conversation (of texting) I had with an online friend I'd only met face to face for a moment and is who'd introduced me to various investments he's involved with.

Question some of you may be asking:

Will Iraq Dinar ever revalue?

Good Question. I don’t know. Have been hoping so.

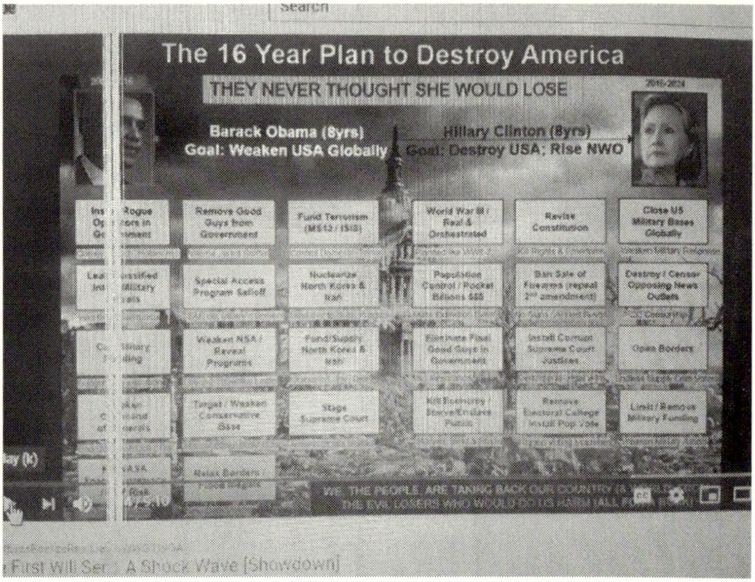

The 16 Year Plan to Destroy America
THEY NEVER THOUGHT SHE WOULD LOSE
Barack Obama (8yrs)
Goal: Weaken USA Globally
Hillary Clinton (8yrs)
Goal: Destroy USA; Rise NWO
Remove Good Guys from Government
Fund Terrorism (MS13 / ISIS)
World War III / Real & Orchestrated
Revise Constitution
Close US Military Bases Globally
Special Access Program Selloff
Nuclearize North Korea & Iran
Population Control / Pocket Billions $$$
Ban Sale of Firearms (repeal 2nd amendment)
Destroy / Censor Opposing News Outlets
Weaken NSA / Reveal Programs
Fund/Supply North Korea & Iran
Eliminate Final Good Guys in Government
Install Corrupt Supreme Court Justices
Open Borders
Target / Weaken Conservative Base
Stage Supreme Court
Kill Economy / Starve/Enslave Public
Remove Electoral College Install Pop Vote
Limit / Remove Military Funding

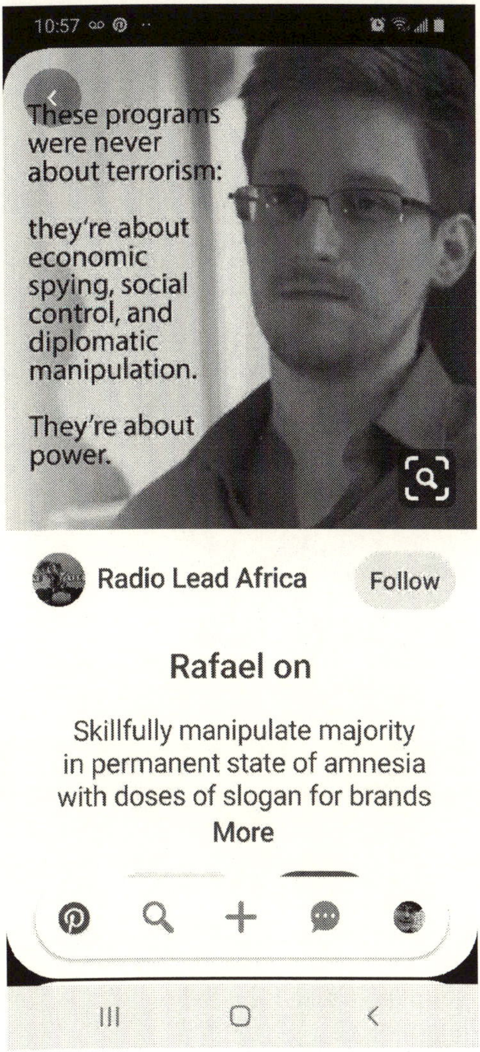
10:57
These programs were never about terrorism:
they're about economic spying, social control, and diplomatic manipulation.
They're about power.
Radio Lead Africa
Follow
Rafael on
Skillfully manipulate majority in permanent state of amnesia with doses of slogan for brands
More

9:34
tumblr
Open in app
POSTS
ASK ME ANYTHING
SO YOU DON'T TRUST THE GOVERNMENT
BUT YOU TRUST NASA
NASA
https://www.nasa.gov
16 notes
flat-earth-memes
flat-earth-memes
Get the Tumblr app
Send
Save

CNN
CHINA'S
NEW WORLD ORDER

CHINA
AND THE
NEW WORLD ORDER

Nancy Pelosi is extremely evil, she comes from the Baltimore democrat corruption machine the D'Alesandro family, both her father Tom D'Alesandro and her brother Tommy D'Alesandro were mayors of Baltimore, a well oiled corrupt democrat family.
– Ronald Reagan 40th President Of The United States

OBAMA AND HILLARY
ASSASSINATED A STATE LEADER
WITHOUT AN ACT OF CONGRESS
OR ANY CRITISM FROM THE MEDIA

CHINA
China respects communism and its leaders

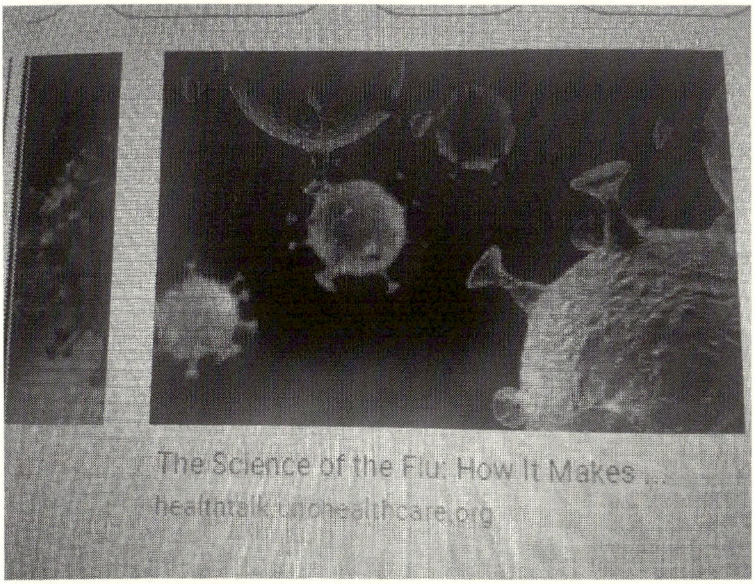
The Science of the Flu: How It Makes ...
healthtalk.unchealthcare.org

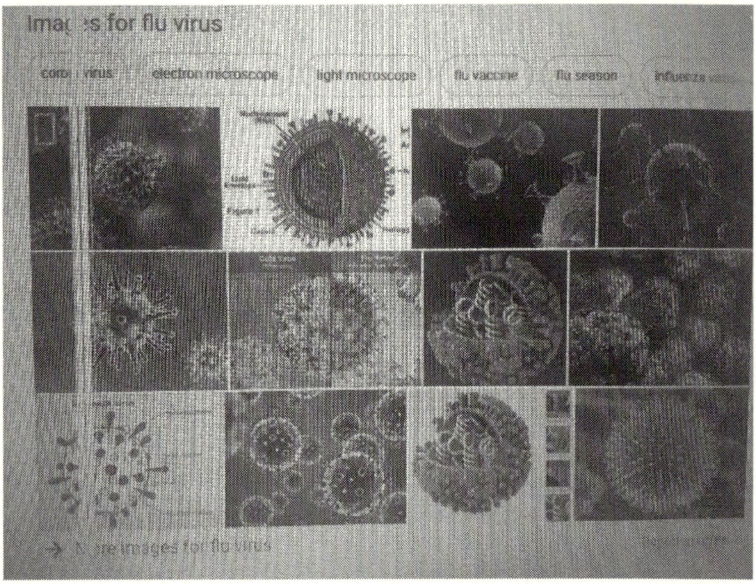
electron microscope
light microscope
flu vaccine
flu season

Whistleblower. Conspiring against the President of the United States of America Donald Trump in an attempt to hurt, damage, and destroy the Constitutional United States. How? In the same way that those who murdered JFK has hurt the USA. And in the same way that those who are behind having prayer taken out of public schools in USA has hurt the country. And in the same way that "Uncle Sam" telling pregnant women that they can murder their children if they choose to has hurt the USA. The same way that 911 has hurt the USA. The same way that ISIS has hurt the USA. The same way that Hillary Clinton and the murder of Epstein has hurt the USA. The same way that Comey and Lynch and Obama have hurt the USA. The same way that Bill Clinton hurt the USA. The same way that Bush and his father and Grandfather hurt the USA. The same way that murdering Bobby Kennedy and Martin Luther King and

Malcom X and Lee Harvey Oswald hurt USA. Etc... Like the way drug cartels in Mexico murdering people hurts USA. The same way that those who are against building a wall along the USA's southern border to regulate those crossing illegally hurts USA. The same way that over 200,000 Christians have been murdered in the last ten years in the

Middle East has hurt USA. Eric Ciaramella is an enemy of the USA laboring with those within the USA who are trying to destroy the USA. There is nothing good about him. He is evil. Propped up by those who hate the USA who are the COMMUNIST within the USA government and the Media and Deep State. Note: Communist = God haters. "They" hate the USA.

2:45
There is only ONE reason
to believe the government's "official" 9/11 story...
Because you blindly trust your government and
have done absolutely no research for yourself.
That's the ONLY reas
From Alien skies under the dome
Alien skies under the dome
Visit
Save
Robert Miller

I WILL SPLINTER THE
CIA INTO A THOUSAN
PIECES AND SCATTER
IT INTO THE WINDS.

templateguru.co • now
Midland: This Anti-Virus N95
Face Mask Can Save Your Life
N95

SECRET
SOVIET STYLE
"INQUIRY"

5/15/67
"Town Meeting of the World"
1967 CBS News Program
REEL AMERICA
AMERICAN HISTORY TV
C-SPAN3

VIVA KENNEDY

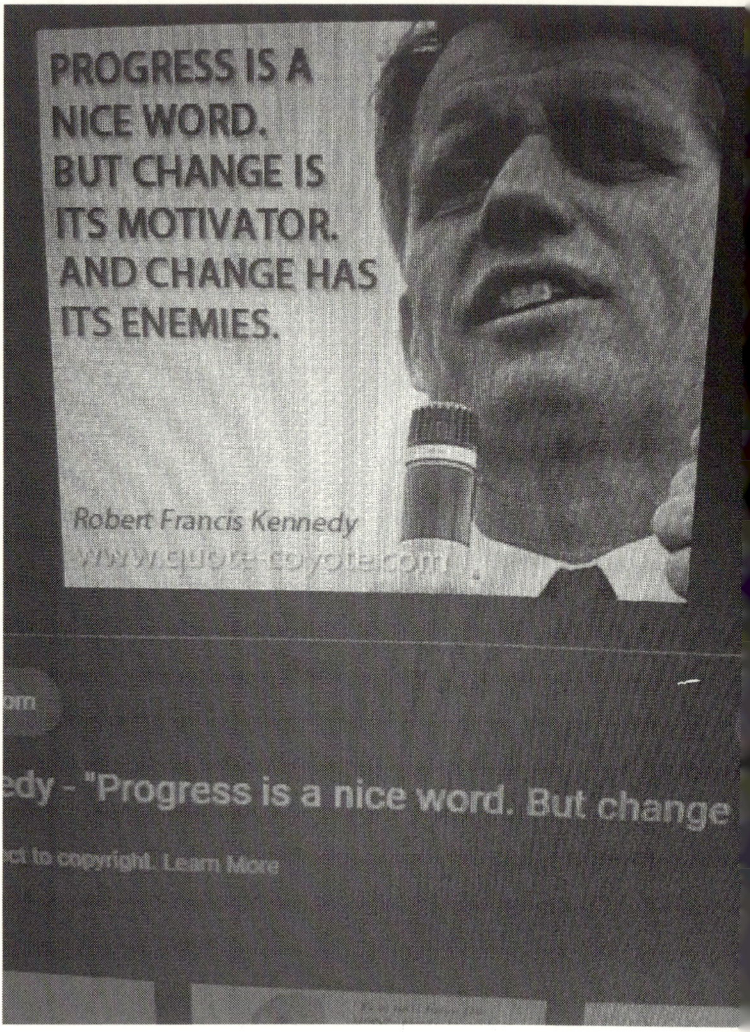
PROGRESS IS A NICE WORD. BUT CHANGE IS ITS MOTIVATOR. AND CHANGE HAS ITS ENEMIES.
Robert Francis Kennedy
www.quote-coyote.com
om
edy - "Progress is a nice word. But change
ect to copyright. Learn More

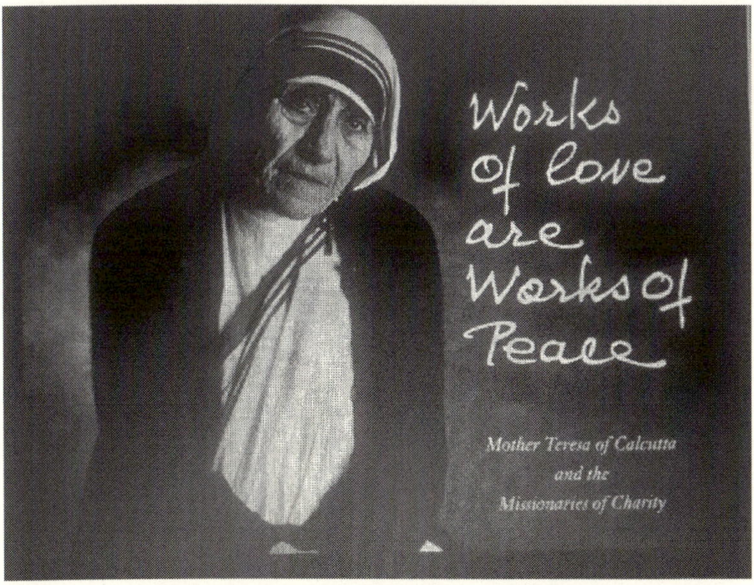
Works
of love
are
Works of
Peace
Mother Teresa of Calcutta
and the
Missionaries of Charity

9:23
Send
Save
Home
Followi...
Create
Notific...
Saved

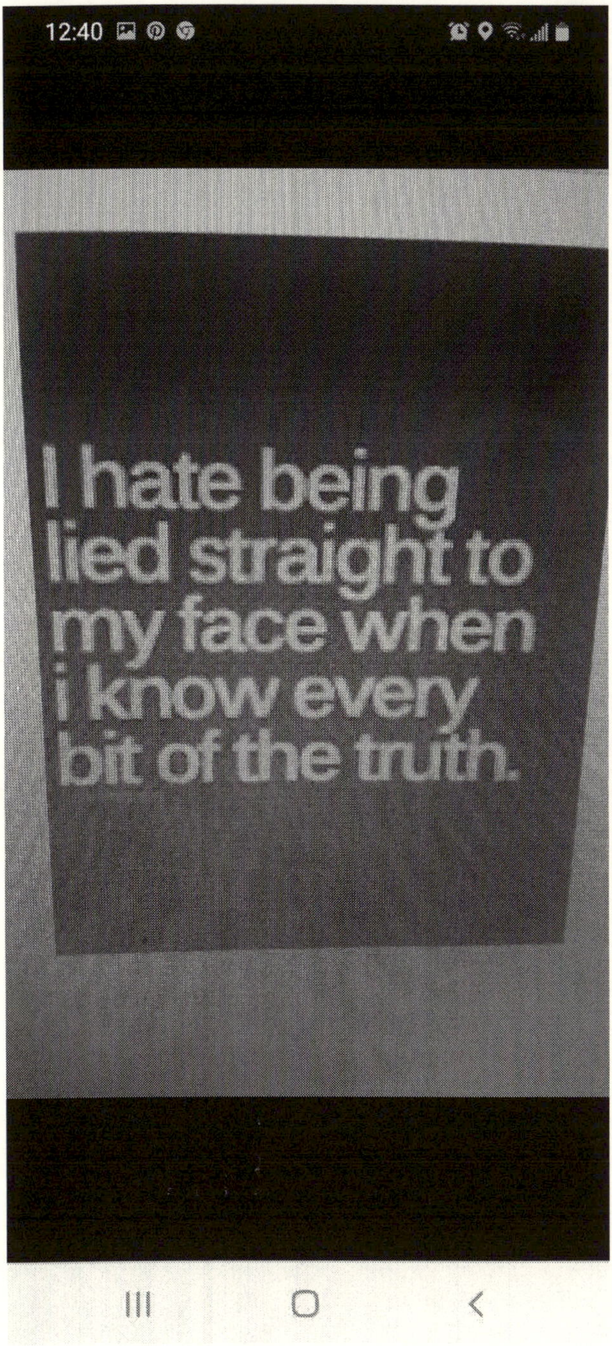
12:40
I hate being
lied straight to
my face when
i know every
bit of the truth.

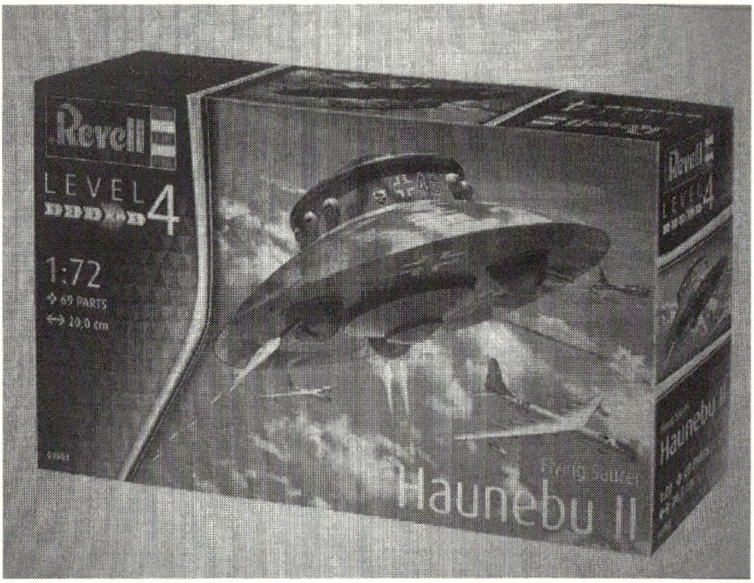
Revell
LEVEL 4
1:72
Flying Saucer
Haunebu II

HERE LIES
HOPE
Global Research

SEVEN YEARS,
GLOBAL PEACE
& THE FALSE
MESSIAH THE
WORLD HAS
ALWAYS WANTED
RETURN OF KING-16

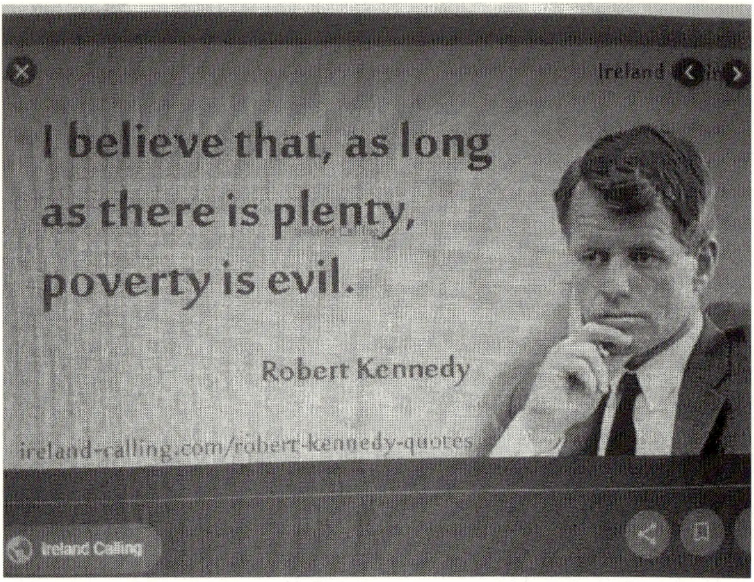
Ireland Calling
I believe that, as long as there is plenty, poverty is evil.
Robert Kennedy
ireland-calling.com/robert-kennedy-quotes
Ireland Calling

Operation High Jump
Antarctica 1946

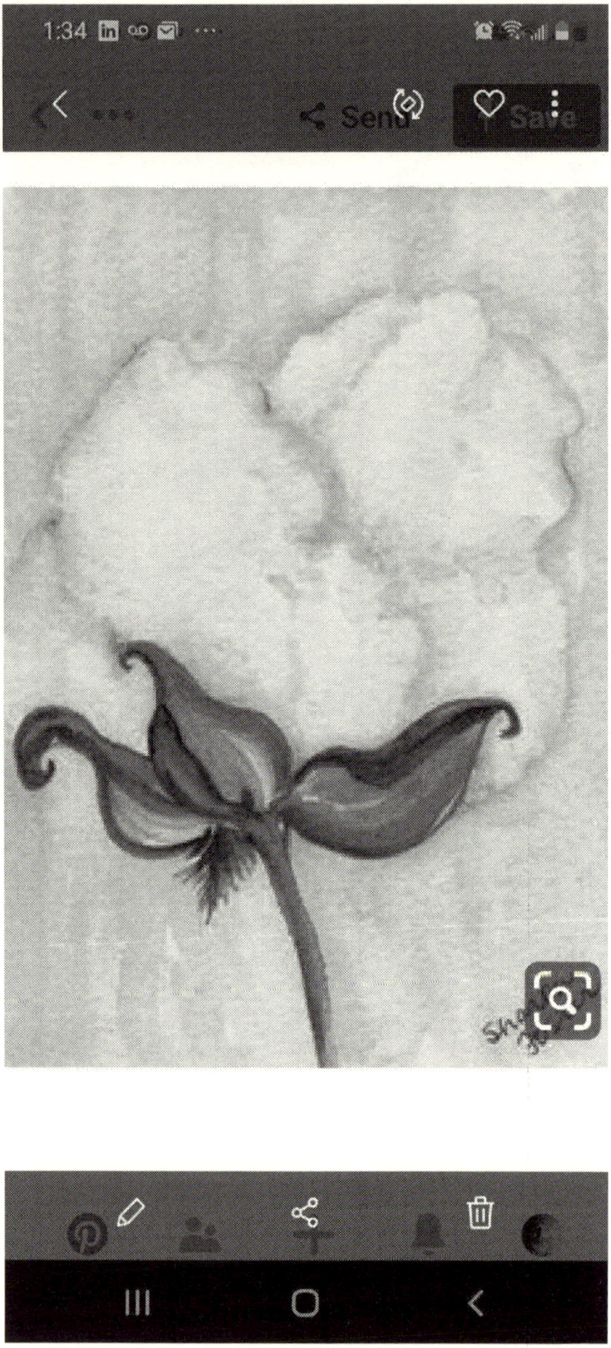
1:34
Send
Save

Space Force
Created to try and stop the one "they" know is coming on the white horse.
Perris Jackson

12:07
Send
Save
Cotton Barn Art Print by Barbel Amos
Home
Followi...
Create
Notific...
Saved

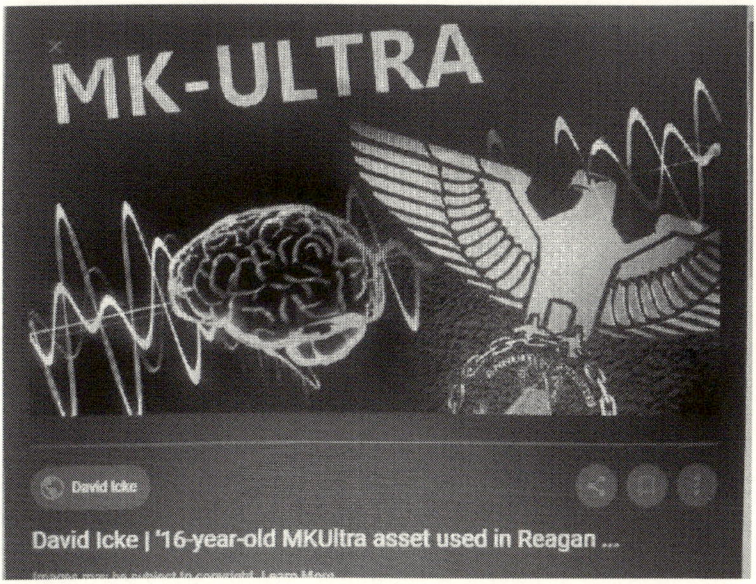

Project MKUltra - Wikipedia
en.wikipedia.org › wiki › Project_MKUltra

Project **MKUltra** (or **M K-Ultra**), also called the CIA mind control program, is the code name given to a program of experiments on human subjects that were designed and undertaken by the U.S. Central Intelligence Agency, some of which were illegal.

A false flag is a covert operation designed to deceive; the deception creates the appearance of a particular party, group, or nation being responsible for some activity, disguising the actual source of responsibility. Wikipedia

FALSE FLAG –
A HORRIFIC, STAGED EVENT - BLAMED ON A POLITICAL ENEMY AND USED AS A PRETEXT TO START A WAR OR ENACT DRACONIAN LAWS IN THE NAME OF NATIONAL SECURITY

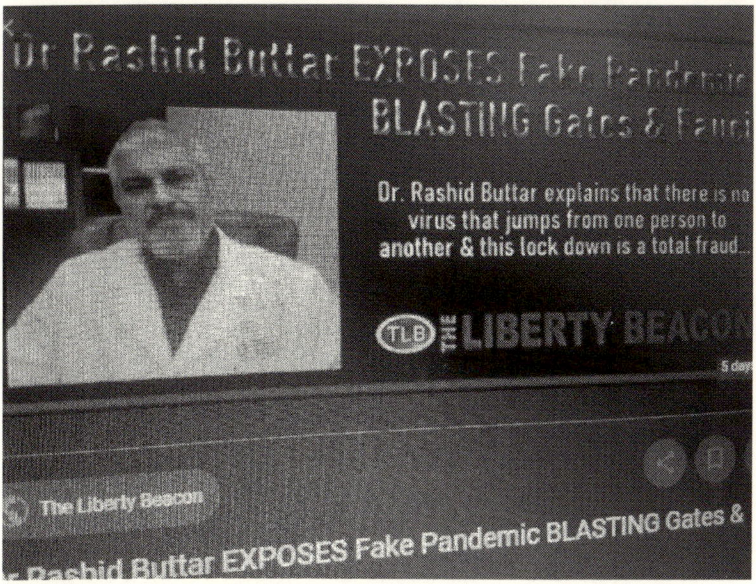

Ask yourself: why has youtube removed the following video and stating that it violates their community standards? What standards are they referring to? Communist standards? For in USA there is freedom of Speech and freedom of Press therefore, what is really going on here when youtube violates Doctor Rashid Buttars USA Constitutional rights? Has he said something wrong?

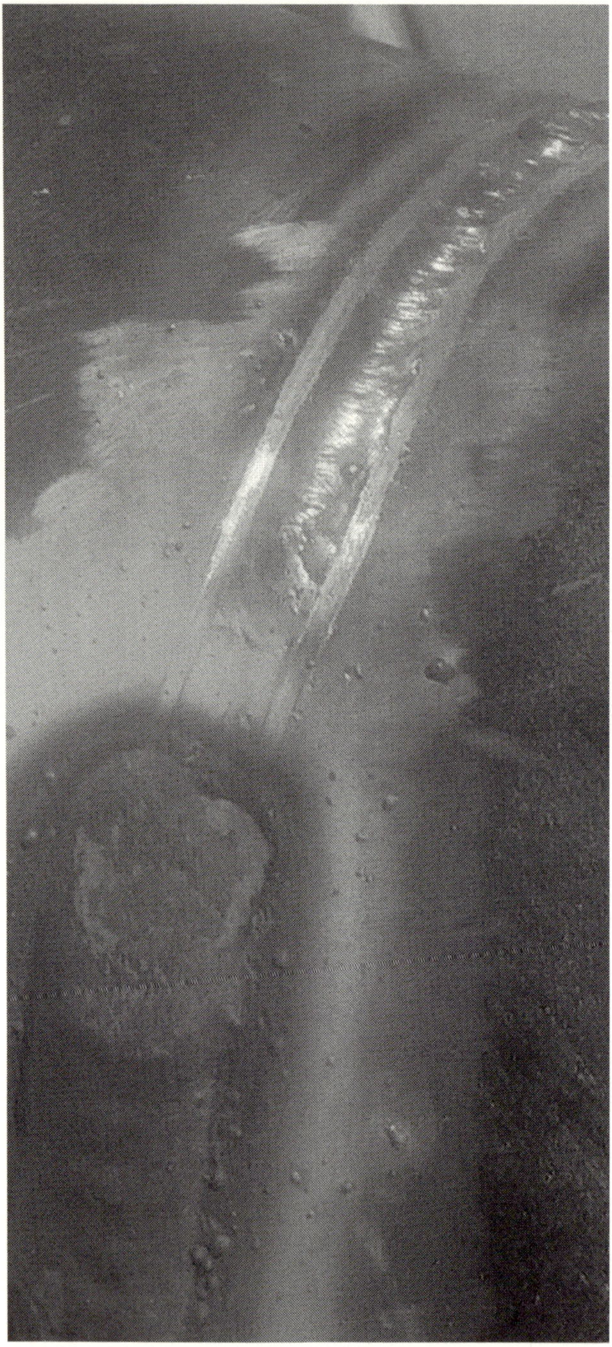

Part 3. Sunrise on a New Day?

It really is the ultimate question you can ask yourself and consequently begin to ask everyone you come in contact with around you. Hey, "Is there going to be a sunrise on a new day for you?" You can ask this question to anyone around you provided that you know the Way. The Way? You may ask.

Yes, the Way, I say. Please listen very carefully because this is a moment of reconciliation for you and your Creator. God is your Creator and He has been separated from this world, this fallen, sinful world ruled by Satan for thousands of years now but God has made a Way for all of mankind to be reconciled to Him if they will only believe on His Way.

His Way is who created all things and by whom all things are held together. His Way is the Son of God. Yes, His own Son who He sacrificed for the sin debt of all mankind so that whoever will believe on Him (God's Son) as the perfect Lamb Sacrificed for the sins of the entire world – they will be saved: Those who believe on Him as their Savior. They, having repented of all their sins before God and accepted the blood of the Lord Jesus Christ to be applied to their sins so that they can live. That’s right, for we have all (the whole world) been dead in our trespasses and sins against God but by Jesus Sacrifice of His life here on Earth the blood that was shed there on the cross that took His Life, that blood can be what covers our sins and makes us righteous in God the Fathers sight and then we have due to having put our belief (faith) in Him (the Lord Jesus Christ to save us) passed from judgement by God unto Life in Christ, because of Christ, And the Lord Jesus Christ didn't stay in the grave but was resurrected by God for His faithfulness to Him (to Father God) and therefore became the Resurrection and because He lives today and forevermore so will we live who have put our trust in Him.

The Bread and the Wine / the Blood of Christ and His Flesh. The Son of God: The Lord Jesus Christ. The One who was dead but is alive forevermore. He is the Way. Trust Him; believe in Him; follow Him; endure until the end and you'll be Saved.

The Apostle John was in Heaven in the Spirit; and he wrote that he heard what sounded like a Lion roaring and then when he turned to see it, that, what he saw was a Lamb that looked as though it had been slain and on Him were the wounds that had once caused His death; and that the Lamb was the Lord Jesus Christ and that He is alive forevermore; Forevermore; yes: FOREVERMORE!!! And in His hands are the Keys of life and death and He is seated at the right hand of the Father and yes, in His hands are the keys of life and death. And He is alive forevermore.

Please hear me, you are in one of two kingdoms. (1.)The kingdom of God where the Lord Jesus Christ is King or (2.) the kingdom of this fallen, cursed world (cursed because of sin…) and ruled by Satan.

…..i.e. which one of these two kingdoms are you in?????

Please be sure and not deceived into thinking that you are in Gods Kingdom and that the Lord Jesus Christ is your Savior if you are not in Gods Kingdom and the Lord Jesus is not your Savior. And with that said, I say this: Please be sure whose kingdom it is that you are truly in right now today; this very moment.

~ Amen. & Amen.

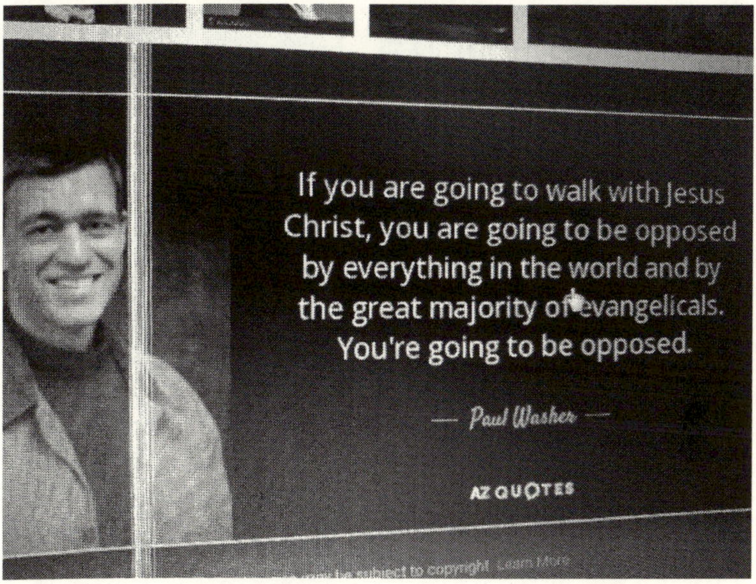
If you are going to walk with Jesus Christ, you are going to be opposed by everything in the world and by the great majority of evangelicals. You're going to be opposed.
— Paul Washer —
AZ QUOTES

"I was thirsty and you gave Me something to drink."
- Matthew 25:35

Luke 22:19 "*The Last Supper*

...18 For I tell you that I will not drink of the fruit of the
vine from now on until the kingdom of God comes." 19
And He took the bread, gave thanks and broke
it, and gave it to
them, saying, "This is My body, given for you; do this i
n remembrance of Me." 20 In the same way, after
supper He took the cup, saying, "This cup is the new
covenant in My blood, which is poured out for you...."

Berean Study Bible ·

Made in the USA
Middletown, DE
07 March 2021

34994363R00076